# sasol

# FIRST FIELD GUIDE TO
# **FROGS**
# OF SOUTHERN AFRICA

Painted Reed Frog

## VINCENT CARRUTHERS

# Contents

| | |
|---|---|
| Introduction | 3 |
| Looking and listening | 4 |
| How to use this book | 6 |
| Species accounts | 8 |
| Glossary | 56 |
| Index | 57 |

*Olive toad*

First published in 2001
by Struik Publishers
(a division of New Holland Publishing
(South Africa) (Pty) Ltd)
80 McKenzie Street,
Cape Town 8001, South Africa

New Holland Publishing is a member of
Johnnic Communications Ltd.
Visit us at www.struik.co.za
Log on to our photographic website
www.imagesofafrica.co.za for an
African experience.

10 9 8 7 6 5 4 3 2

Copyright © text: V Carruthers 2001
Copyright © photographs:
V Carruthers 2001
Copyright © maps and illustrations:
Struik Publishers 2001

Copyright © published edition:
Struik Publishers 2001

All rights reserved. No part of this
publication may be reproduced, stored
in a retrieval system or transmitted,
in any form or by any means,
electronic, mechanical, photocopying,
recording or otherwise, without the
prior written permission of the
copyright holders.

Publishing Manager: Pippa Parker
Managing Editor: Helen de Villiers
Editor: Sally Woudberg
Designer: Dominic Robson

Reproduction: Scan Shop
Printed and bound by Paarl Print

ISBN 1 86872 595 2

# Introduction

Everyone can recognize a frog. They are common and harmless, they do not destroy crops or property nor do they transmit human disease; yet they are often despised and sometimes even feared. This book tries to correct these perceptions by introducing some of the fascinating aspects of frog life in southern Africa.

Frogs are amphibians, a group of animals that has two stages to their lives – first as an aquatic[G] tadpole and then a terrestrial[G] frog (amphi = two, bios = life).

Metamorphosis[G] from tadpole to frog is one of the wonders of nature. In a matter of days the tadpole develops limbs, a skeleton and the ability to walk or hop, call, breed, hunt insects and breathe air. In short, it becomes a totally different creature.

Amphibians evolved from fish about 350 million years ago. They were the first vertebrate[G] animals to inhabit the land and they were the ancestors, not only of modern frogs, but also of all reptiles, birds and mammals, including ourselves.

The terms 'frog' and 'toad' are sometimes confusing. Toads are one of many families of frogs, just as ducks are one family of birds. Some other examples of frog families include river and stream frogs, tree frogs and rain frogs.

*Metamorphosis; change from tadpole to frog*

# Looking and Listening

*Olive Toad calling*

## Frog Calls

Most frogs are nocturnal and therefore more often heard than seen. Males call to attract females to the breeding site. The sound is made by blowing air over the vocal chords into a vocal sac$^G$ that resonates loudly. Each species$^G$ has its own unique mating call and the female responds only to a male of her own species. The mating call is the way frogs identify themselves, so it is the best way for us to identify them. Learning to distinguish between the different calls is fun and rewarding.

### WHEN

Frogs are most active in the rainy season – summer time in most of southern Africa or late winter and early spring in the Western Cape. This is because moisture is essential for frog survival. Their skin is porous and they soon die if allowed to dry out. They also need fresh water or damp places in which to lay their eggs. The best time to find frogs is after dark when you can track their calls.

### WHERE

Frogs occur throughout southern Africa, even in the Namib Desert. However, they generally prosper in localities that are warm and damp. A glance at the distribution maps on the following pages will show that the greatest number of species are found in the east of the region where high rainfall combines with warm year-round temperatures. In humid, coastal localities as many as 20 different species may be found at a single pan$^G$.

The best places to look for frogs are the shallow edges of pans<sup>G</sup> and ponds, the banks of streams and wet moss or decaying leaves in forests. Each species<sup>G</sup> has very particular habitat<sup>G</sup> preferences and, even at a single pan, different species will be confined to certain localities such as reed beds, flooded grassland or mud banks.

## HOW

You will need a torch, insect repellant and plenty of patience because frogs usually remain well concealed and calls sometimes seem to be ventriloqual. Approach the calling frogs

*Looking for frogs in the shallows*

slowly. If they are disturbed and stop calling, wait motionlessly until they start up again.

The fun of frog watching comes from observing their behaviour: watch how males defend their call sites and how different species have developed interesting ways to keep their eggs and tadpoles safe from predators and adverse weather. Observe the drama of hunting and being hunted – frogs consume huge numbers of insects and they themselves fall prey to birds, snakes, other frogs and even fishing spiders.

*An ideal wetland site for frogs*

# How to use this book

The purpose of this book is to introduce amateur naturalists to species[G] of frogs that are likely to be encountered, and to aid in identifying them. Each species or group of species has a page of information, together with a colour photograph and a map showing where it is found.

Each species account contains a series of headings as follows:

**Size:** This is the distance from the tip of the snout to the end of the body (i.e. excluding the legs). The average size of an adult is given. Some individuals may be slightly smaller or bigger. The millimetre scale on the back cover will assist in judging the size of the frog.

**Description:** The overall shape, colour and identifying features of the frog are given. Colour is not always a reliable feature as frogs of the same species often vary. The extent to which colour can vary in each case is noted.

**Where found:** Type of habitat[G] and the vegetation are useful clues to identification.

**Call:** If heard, this is a very reliable way of identifying a frog.

**Reproduction:** Eggs and tadpoles of the species are described. Breeding behaviour is always interesting to observe.

**Notes:** Interesting facts about each frog are given.

**Distribution map:** Ensure that your specimen was found in the range shown on the map.

### Handling the specimen

To identify a frog you may have to catch it and place it temporarily in a clear plastic bag. Inflate the bag so the frog can be seen clearly through the taut plastic. Frogs are extremely delicate so handle them gently and, once identified, always release them in the same place they were found.

*Ready for identification*

## IDENTIFYING A FROG

Ask these questions:
- What is the overall shape of the frog?
- Is the skin smooth or does it bear glandular<sup>G</sup> lumps or ridges?
- Is there an oval-shape, elevated lump behind the eye? (This is called a parotid gland<sup>G</sup> and is characteristic of toads.)
- Are the legs longer or shorter than the body?
- Is there webbing between the toes for swimming?
- Are there adhesive pads at the tips of the toes for climbing?

- Is there a digging tubercle<sup>G</sup> on the heel?

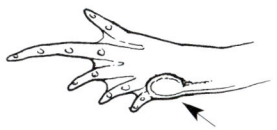

- Do any of the toes bear hard claws?

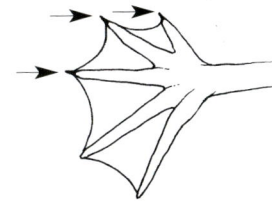

- In bright light, is the pupil of the eye:

vertically elliptical?

horizontally elliptical?

or circular?

# Bush Squeaker

*Arthroleptis wahlbergi*

**Size:** 25–40 mm.

**Description:** Stocky body. Brown or grey above with a pattern of interlinked diamond shapes down the back. Top of snout paler than the body. Belly is granular<sup>G</sup> white with dark flecks. Toes without webbing. Pupils horizontal.

**Where found:** In forests in fallen leaves or decaying vegetation.

**Call:** Long, high-pitched squeak repeated continuously during rain or mist.

**Reproduction:** Eggs scattered among damp leaf litter. Tadpoles remain in the egg capsule until they metamorphose<sup>G</sup> into 3 mm miniature frogs.

**Notes:** It can be very difficult to find on the forest floor. The squeaking call is often mistaken for that of an insect. Specimens found in the south are larger than those from KwaZulu-Natal.

# Sand Toad

*Bufo angusticeps*

**Size:** 40–60 mm.

**Description:** Thickset body covered in rounded bumps with parotid glands<sup>G</sup> behind the eyes. Grey with pairs of irregularly shaped dark patches on the back and a narrow vertebral<sup>G</sup> stripe. One pair of dark patches on the snout and another behind the eyes. Belly granular<sup>G</sup> white but smooth on throat. Toes have a fringe of webbing. Upper surface of feet yellow. Pupils horizontal.

**Where found:** Around wetlands in sandy areas with coastal fynbos<sup>G</sup>.

**Call:** A soft, nasal bray with long intervals in between each call.

**Reproduction:** Strings of eggs are laid during winter in temporary, rain-filled depressions. Tadpoles reach 22 mm; black with white fins. Metamorphosis<sup>G</sup> is complete by the end of August.

**Notes:** Although it was once common in the Western Cape, the destruction of its habitat<sup>G</sup> through housing and industrial development is now threatening this species<sup>G</sup>.

# Pygmy Toads

*Bufo* sp.

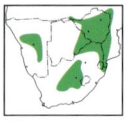

**This group includes:** Beira Pygmy Toad, *Bufo beiranus;* Northern Pygmy Toad, *Bufo fenoulheti;* Southern Pygmy Toad, *Bufo vertebralis*

**Size:** 25–35 mm.

**Description:** Slight, rough-skinned body with flat parotid glands<sup>G</sup>. Mottled grey or brown with reddish markings and a pale patch between the shoulders. Belly granular<sup>G</sup> white with a few black spots. Toes without webbing. Pupils horizontal.

**Where found:** Rocky outcrops in grassland or savanna<sup>G</sup>.

**Call:** Harsh chirping sounds, similar to those made by a cricket.

**Reproduction:** Strings of eggs laid in exposed, rain-filled rock pools. Tadpoles reach 21 mm and metamorphose<sup>G</sup> in less than three weeks in order to avoid being trapped in a drying pool.

**Notes:** Different species<sup>G</sup> are found in different localities. The Beira Pygmy Toad is thought to be the smallest toad in the world (*Guinness Book of Records*).

*Southern Pygmy Toad*

# Karoo Toad

*Bufo gariepensis*

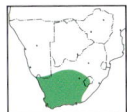

**Size:** 70–90 mm.

**Description:** Thickset body covered in rounded bumps. Parotid glands<sup>G</sup> prominent behind the eyes. Tan coloured with asymmetrical dark brown patches. Belly off-white, young frogs' bellies often covered in spots. Toes have barely any webbing. Pupils horizontal.

**Where found:** Around dams and temporary streams in open grassland or scrub. Forages some distance away from water.

**Call:** A series of rasping squawks by day or night.

**Reproduction:** Strings of eggs are laid in shallow pools in stream beds and at the edges of farm dams. Tadpoles black; reach 25 mm and cluster together in loose shoals.

**Notes:** Common throughout the Karoo. Similar frogs have been recorded in Swaziland but are likely to be another species<sup>G</sup>.

# Olive Toads

*Bufo* sp.

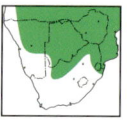

**This group includes:**
Eastern Olive Toad, *Bufo garmani;* Western Olive Toad, *Bufo poweri*

**Size:** 80–100 mm.

**Description:** Heavy body with rough, lumpy skin. Bears large parotid glands<sup>G</sup>. Pairs of dark patches are present down the back but not on the snout,. A pale vertebral<sup>G</sup> stripe occasionally present from behind the head. Belly is granular<sup>G</sup> white, with a dark throat in males. Red blotches appear on the inner legs. Toes have very little webbing. Pupils horizontal.

**Where found:** Dams and pans<sup>G</sup> in open woodland savanna<sup>G</sup>. Forages away from water.

**Call:** A loud, rasping bray, often in a chorus.

**Reproduction:** Breeding begins in early spring. Strings of eggs are draped around underwater vegetation and tadpoles metamorphose<sup>G</sup> with the first rains. Tadpoles reach 25 mm; black with gold specks.

**Notes:** It is common throughout the range and is often found around the camps in bushveld<sup>G</sup> game parks.

*Western Olive Toad*

# Guttural Toad

*Bufo gutturalis*

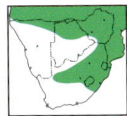

**Size:** 80–100 mm.

**Description:** Heavy body with rough, lumpy skin and large parotid glands<sup>G</sup>. Pairs of dark patches down the back, including a pair on the snout and another behind the eyes, leaving a pale cross shape on the head. A vertebral<sup>G</sup> stripe occasionally present. Belly granular<sup>G</sup> white, with a dark throat in males. Inner legs have red blotches. Toes have barely any webbing. Pupils horizontal.

**Where found:** Around dams, pans<sup>G</sup> and streams in grassland and savanna<sup>G</sup>. Forages away from water and readily inhabits suburban gardens.

**Call:** A deep, vibrant snore, usually in large choruses.

**Reproduction:** Breeding begins in spring. Strings of eggs are laid in permanent water such as dams or ponds in river backwaters where tadpoles feed on algae along the edges. Tadpoles reach 25 mm; black with gold specks.

**Notes:** Because it has adapted so easily to man-made ponds and gardens, it is one of the most commonly seen frogs in the urban areas within its range. Individuals frequently wait around electric lights to catch and feed on visiting insects.

# Leopard Toads

*Bufo* sp.

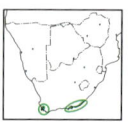

**This group includes:** Eastern Leopard Toad, *Bufo pardalis*; Western Leopard Toad, *Bufo pantherinus*

**Size:** 100–140 mm.

**Description:** Large, heavy body with granular<sup>G</sup>, lumpy skin and large parotid glands<sup>G</sup>. Pairs of red-brown patches on the back, outlined in yellow in the Western Leopard Toad. A narrow vertebral<sup>G</sup> stripe often present. Belly granular white, with a dark throat in males. Toes have a margin of webbing. Pupils horizontal.

**Where found:** Around dams or other permanent water situated in fynbos<sup>G</sup> or grassland. Calls when in concealed positions or while in deep water away from the bank.

**Call:** A low, slow, growling snore that is repeated at well-spaced intervals.

**Reproduction:** Breeds during August in deep, permanent water such as dams. Tadpoles reach 30 mm; black.

**Notes:** Secretive and seldom seen except during August, which is its breeding season. The two species<sup>G</sup> occur in localities that are separated by many kilometres.

*Western Leopard Toad*

# Raucous Toad

*Bufo rangeri*

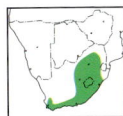

**Size:** 80–100 mm.

**Description:** Thickset body with rough, lumpy skin and large parotid glands<sup>G</sup>. Pairs of dark patches run down the back, those behind the eyes are joined into a single bar across the head. No patches appear on the snout. Occasionally a vertebral<sup>G</sup> stripe, starting from between the shoulders. Belly granular<sup>G</sup> white, with a dark throat in males. Some webbing is present between the base of the toes. No digging tubercle<sup>G</sup>. Pupils horizontal.

**Where found:** Grassland and fynbos<sup>G</sup> near rivers and streams. Calls from river banks.

**Call:** Short, rasping, duck-like quacks rapidly repeated. Males call singly or in small groups, seldom in large choruses.

**Reproduction:** Eggs are laid in the still reaches of rivers, streams and man-made ponds. Tadpoles reach 25 mm; black with gold specks.

**Notes:** Often hybridises<sup>G</sup> with Guttural Toads, especially in artificial dams, ponds and ornamental water features. Only a small proportion of the hybrid offspring survive and they have a call pitched midway between that of the Raucous Toad and the Guttural Toad.

# Mountain Toads

*Capensibufo* sp.

**This group includes:** Rose's Mountain Toad, *Capensibufo rosei*; Tradouw Mountain Toad, *Capensibufo tradouwi*

**Size:** 30–35 mm.

**Description:** Slightly elongated, smooth bodies with small, blister-like bumps on the skin. Parotid glands<sup>G</sup> and other elevations have a red or orange colour. Belly has grey, mottled markings and is granular<sup>G</sup> at the rear. Toes without webbing. Pupils horizontal.

**Where found:** Vleis<sup>G</sup> and moist slopes in mountain fynbos<sup>G</sup>.

**Call:** Rose's Mountain Toad does not appear to call. The Tradouw Mountain Toad has a creaking squawk ending in a sharp squeak.

**Reproduction:** Large groups gather in shallow, rain-filled depressions to breed in early spring. Eggs are laid in jelly which is constricted between each egg like beads on a string. Tadpoles reach 20 mm, black.

**Notes:** The apparent absence of a mating call makes Rose's Mountain Toad extremely unusual.

*Tradouw Mountain Toad*

# Red Toad

*Schismaderma carens*

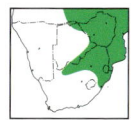

**Size:** 70–90 mm.

**Description:** Body leathery without lumps or parotid glands^G. Reddish brown with two dark spots in the middle of the back. A dark ridge along each flank. Belly granular^G with small dark specks. Male throat is wrinkled. Toes have a noticeable margin of webbing. Pupils horizontal.

**Where found:** Favours farm dams and pans^G in grassland and savanna^G but forages far from water. Retreats into holes in trees during the day.

**Call:** Males call while floating; a long, deep, booming call; usually in choruses. Calls after rains by day and night.

**Reproduction:** Breeds in deep water during the rainy season. Tadpoles swim just below the surface and form dense, football-sized shoals. Tadpoles reach 35 mm; black with skin flap on the head.

**Notes:** Common within its range, both in the wild and in suburban gardens and is often found in swimming pools. It is a friend to gardeners as it consumes rose-beetles and other garden pests and is itself the favoured food of night adders.

# Ghost Frogs

*Heleophryne* sp.

**This group includes:**
Cape Ghost Frog, *Heleophryne purcelli*;
Hewitt's Ghost Frog, *Heleophryne hewitti*;
Natal Ghost Frog, *Heleophryne natalensis*;
Southern Ghost Frog, *Heleophryne regis*;
Table Mountain Ghost Frog, *Heleophryne rosei*

**Size:** 40–60 mm.

**Description:** Slightly flattened head and body. Slippery-skinned with bulging eyes and long limbs. Greenish-brown with deep reddish mottling or patches. Natal Ghost Frog has yellow markings on a dark brown background. Belly granular[G] white. Toes with T-shaped adhesive pads and extensive webbing. Pupils vertical.

**Where found:** Fast-flowing mountain streams, in forests.

*Cape Ghost Frog*

**Call:** Clear, high-pitched ringing or whistling notes, audible above the rushing stream.

**Reproduction:** Eggs are laid in protected places next to mountain streams. Tadpoles are adapted to the fast-flowing water and cling to rocks with their teeth while eating the algae. Tadpoles live for two seasons and grow to 90 mm before they metamorphose[G].

**Notes:** The highly specialised tadpoles are able to climb vertical waterfalls using their teeth to grip onto the slippery rocks. Different species[G] inhabit different isolated regions.

# Shovel-nosed Frogs

*Hemisus* sp.

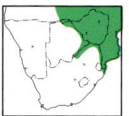

**This group includes:** Spotted Shovel-nosed Frog, *Hemisus guttatus;* Mottled Shovel-nosed Frog, *Hemisus marmoratus*

**Size:** 40–70 mm.

**Description:** Rotund body with smooth skin. Has small eyes and a hard, chisel-like snout used for digging. Brown with yellow mottling or spots. Belly is smooth, pinkish-white. Male has a dark throat. Toes have little or no webbing and heel has no digging tubercle[G]. Pupils vertical.

**Where found:** Burrows in muddy banks of coastal savanna[G] pans[G] and slow-moving streams. Seldom found above ground.

**Call:** Calls from within the burrow; long, incessant insect-like trills. Especially vocal during rain.

**Reproduction:** Eggs are laid underground. The female carries the hatchling tadpoles along a burrow to the water. Tadpoles grow to 55 mm; base of tail dark, tip colourless.

**Notes:** One of the few frogs that tunnel headfirst using its snout as a spade. Most other burrowing species[G] use a tubercle on their heels to dig backwards.

*Mottled Shovel-nosed Frog*

# Dwarf Leaf-folding Frogs

*Afrixalus* sp.

**This group includes:**
Delicate Leaf-folding Frog, *Afrixalus delicatus*;
Golden Leaf-folding Frog, *Afrixalus aureus*;
Knysna Leaf-folding Frog, *Afrixalus knysnae*;
Natal Leaf-folding Frog, *Afrixalus spinifrons*;
Snoring Leaf-folding Frog, *Afrixalus crotalus*

**Size:** 20–22 mm

**Description:** Elongated, golden-yellow body, sometimes partly covered with minute black asperities<sup>G</sup>. Flanks brown with white stipples<sup>G</sup>. Some species<sup>G</sup> have a wide brown stripe down the centre of the back. Belly cream. Male throat yellow. Toes webbed with adhesive discs. Pupils vertical.

**Where found:** Savanna<sup>G</sup> pans<sup>G</sup> with grassy shallows or inundated vegetation.

*Golden Leaf-folding Frog*

**Call:** Sharp zips and buzzing sounds not audible from afar.

**Reproduction:** Eggs are laid along the length of a grass-leaf that is then folded and glued into a protective tube. When the tadpoles hatch the glue dissolves and they swim freely away; 30 mm and colourless with a dark patch on head.

**Notes:** Sometimes a male will silently wait near another calling male and intercept any approaching female to mate with her.

# Greater Leaf-folding Frog

*Afrixalus fornasinii*

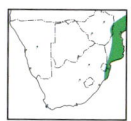

**Size:** 30–40 mm.

**Description:** Elongated, cream or yellow body with a central brown stripe coming to a point between the eyes. Covered with white specks and asperities<sup>G</sup>. Flanks brown with white stipples<sup>G</sup>. Belly granular<sup>G</sup> cream. Male has a yellow throat. Toes webbed with adhesive discs. Pupils vertical.

**Where found:** Savanna<sup>G</sup> pans<sup>G</sup> with grassy shallows. Retreats into the axils of wild banana leaves during the day.

**Call:** A rapid burst of loud, percussive 'shots'.

**Reproduction:** Eggs are laid on a leaf several centimetres above the water. The leaf is folded and glued into a protective envelope. When the tadpoles hatch they slither into the water; 30 mm, dark above and white below.

**Notes:** They are similar in shape and size to some Reed Frogs, but are distinguishable by their vertical eyes.

# Bubbling Kassina

*Kassina senegalensis*

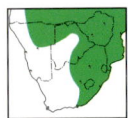

**Size:** 30–50 mm.

**Description:** Smooth-skinned, bullet-shaped body. Cream to olive with solid wide dark stripe down the centre of the back and broken stripes down the sides and flanks. Belly smooth, white. Male throat dark. Toes barely webbed. Pupils vertical.

**Where found:** Grassland vleis<sup>G</sup>; open savanna<sup>G</sup>.

**Call:** A clear, liquid 'quoip' every few seconds.

**Reproduction:** Eggs are layed in individual jelly capsules and attached to underwater plants. The tadpoles are beautiful; up to 80 mm long with wide, colourful tail fins.

**Notes:** Males start calling in the grassland during the mid-afternoon and move to the water's edge as night starts to approach. Although the call is a familiar sound to many people, it is difficult to locate the frog precisely due to its bubbling quality. Bubbling Kassinas seldom hop, but tend to walk or run on their spindly legs and are therefore sometimes referred to as 'Running Frogs' in certain reference books.

# Rattling Frog

*Semnodactylus wealli*

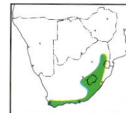

**Size:** 35–45 mm.

**Description:** Smooth-skinned, stocky body. Cream with dark stripes down the back and sides. Each stripe is divided longitudinally, showing a pale background colour along the centre. Belly is coarsely granular[G] white. Male has a dark throat. Toes are barely webbed with no adhesive discs. Pupils vertical.

**Where found:** Vleis[G] and inundated grassland. Calls from thick vegetation in shallow water.

**Call:** A coarse, loud rattling.

**Reproduction:** Eggs in individual jelly capsules are attached to underwater plants. Tadpoles reach 60 mm; speckled brown.

**Notes:** Like the Bubbling Kassina, these frogs are sometimes called 'Running Frogs' because of their inclination to run rather than hop. When handled or molested they often sham dead until there is an opportunity to scurry away to safety.

# Arum Lily Reed Frog

*Hyperolius horstockii*

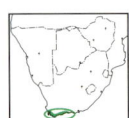

**Size:** 35–40 mm.

**Where found:** Sedges and lilies around pans<sup>G</sup> in fynbos<sup>G</sup>.

**Call:** A continuous, nasal bleat.

**Description:** Smooth skinned. Putty coloured. A pale stripe, underscored with minute spots, runs from the snout along the flanks. Belly is granular<sup>G</sup> cream. Male has an orange throat. Toes are webbed, orange-pink with adhesive discs. Pupils horizontal.

**Reproduction:** Eggs are attached to underwater plants in clusters of about a dozen. Tadpoles reach 40 mm; brown stripes on a spotted background.

**Notes:** Often waits in the cup of an arum lily to ambush insects that visit the flower.

# Painted Reed Frog

*Hyperolius marmoratus*

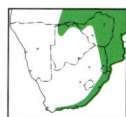

**Size:** 25–35 mm.

**Description:** Smooth-skinned. Many different patterns, often brightly coloured, from spotted to striped or marbled[G]. Belly is granular[G] white or pink. Male has a grey throat, sometimes with orange spots. Inner limbs and toes bright pink. Toes are webbed and bear adhesive discs. Pupils horizontal.

**Where found:** Reed beds at the edges of savanna[G] pans[G]. By day they rest in the canopy of trees.

**Call:** Short, loud, piercing whistles – about one per second – often in large choruses.

**Reproduction:** Batches of about 10 eggs are deposited on submerged plants or stones. Tadpoles reach 45 mm; brown speckled with a black tip that varies in extent from one tadpole to another.

**Notes:** The bright colours fade during daylight and frogs sit in exposed positions with their feet tucked under their bodies.

# Waterlily Reed Frog

*Hyperolius pusillus*

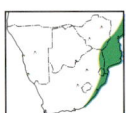

**Size:** 18–20 mm.

**Description:** Smooth-skinned. Translucent green, sometimes with stipples<sup>G</sup> or very indistinct stripes. Blunt snout. Belly smooth white or transparent. Males have a yellow throat. Inner limbs and toes translucent blue-green. Toes webbed with adhesive discs. Pupils horizontal.

**Where found:** Waterlily pads or other floating vegetation among reed beds situated around lowveld<sup>G</sup> pans<sup>G</sup>.

**Call:** A blurred, extremely high-pitched tick at the highest range that is audible to human ears.

**Reproduction:** Eggs are laid between overlapping waterlily pads and the leaves are glued together to protect the eggs. Tadpoles reach 35 mm; pale greenish-brown striped with a black tip to the tail.

**Notes:** Males call while sitting on waterlilies and constantly chivvy and chase about while punching each other with their vocal sacs.

# Yellow-striped Reed Frog

*Hyperolius semidiscus*

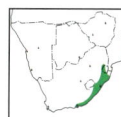

**Size:** 30–35 mm.

**Description:** Smooth-skinned. Green or brown. Yellow stripes with thin black borders along the flanks, sometimes extending to the snout. Belly granular<sup>G</sup> cream or yellow. Male has a dark yellow throat. Inner limbs and toes orange or yellow. Toes webbed with adhesive discs. Pupils horizontal.

**Where found:** Reeds on edges of grassland rivers and pans<sup>G</sup>.

**Call:** A harsh creaking interspersed with longer, vibrating croaks.

**Reproduction:** Eggs are laid on underwater vegetation in clusters of about 50. Tadpoles reach 48 mm; mottled brown with a white belly.

**Notes:** Individuals are able to change colour from green to brown, depending on their surroundings and levels of stress. Individuals from the northern part of the range are usually slightly larger than those found in the south.

# Tinker Reed Frog

*Hyperolius tuberilinguis*

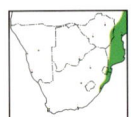

**Size:** 30–35 mm.

**Description:** Smooth-skinned. Plain opaque green, yellow or brown. Belly granular[G] cream. Males throat yellow. Inner limbs and toes orange or yellow. Toes webbed with adhesive discs. Pupils horizontal.

**Where found:** Concealed positions among reeds and other vegetation at the edges of coastal pans[G]. Often inhabits garden fishponds in Durban.

**Call:** Two rapid, staccato taps (or occasionally a series of several taps) in less than a second, with long intervals in between each call.

**Reproduction:** Several hundred eggs are laid in a stiff jelly cake on vegetation a few centimetres above the water. Tadpoles reach 45 mm; brown with a white belly and a tail bearing longitudinal dark stripes.

**Notes:** Constantly on the move, chivvying each other while calling and feeding voraciously on mosquitoes.

# Argus Reed Frog

*Hyperolius argus*

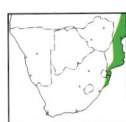

**Size:** 30–35 mm.

**Description:** Smooth-skinned. Purplish brown or green. Yellow stripes with thick black border running from the snout to the eyes in females, extending onto flanks as stripes or rows of dots in males. Belly granular[G] white or yellow in males, smooth and translucent in females. Male throat granular yellow. Inner limbs and toes brown or orange. Toes webbed with adhesive discs. Pupils horizontal.

**Where found:** Low reeds near the water surface or floating vegetation at the edges of lowveld[G] coastal pans[G].

**Call:** Rapidly repeated clucks.

**Reproduction:** Eggs laid in clusters underwater. Tadpoles reach 45 mm; speckled brown with a white belly.

*Female*

**Notes:** One of few species[G] in which the male and female frogs differ noticeably.

*Male*

# Brown-backed Tree Frog

*Leptopelis mossambicus*

**Size:** 50–60 mm.

**Description:** Stocky body with broad head and slightly granular[G] skin. Tan with distinct brown horseshoe pattern on the back. Juveniles plain green. Belly granular white. Toes with adhesive discs and very little webbing. Digging tubercle[G] on the heel. Pupils vertical.

**Where found:** In trees around pans[G] in open woodland savanna[G]. Burrows into the sand by day.

**Call:** A loud double 'yack-yack', often preceded by a soft buzzing.

**Reproduction:** Eggs are laid on banks adjacent to the water. Tadpoles reach 60 mm; black with darkly speckled tail fins.

**Notes:** In winter Brown-backed Trees Frogs bury themselves about 500 mm underground to avoid dehydrating during the dry season. They lie there motionlessly for several months. A secretion from their skin sets into a thin membrane, completely sealing their whole bodies, except for their nostrils.

# Forest Tree Frog

*Leptopelis natalensis*

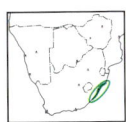

**Size:** 45–55 mm.

**Description:** Stocky body with slightly granular<sup>G</sup> skin. Plain leaf-green or cream. Juveniles are brown with green patches. Belly granular white. Toes webbed with adhesive discs. No digging tubercle<sup>G</sup> on the heel. Pupils vertical.

**Where found:** Trees, shrubs near streams in forest and coastal bush.

**Call:** A loud 'yack', often preceded by a soft buzzing.

**Reproduction:** Eggs are laid on banks adjacent to the water. On hatching, tadpoles squirm in a mass down to the water. They reach 50 mm; dark grey or brown except for the lower tail fin which is transparent.

**Notes:** Hunts insects at night by jumping from branch to branch.

Males wrestle with one another to secure a calling site in a tree. Their limbs and toes are spread wide as they leap and when any adhesive toe pad makes contact with a leaf or branch the frog is swung around onto it.

# Forest Rain Frogs

*Breviceps* sp.

**This group includes:**
Plain Rain Frog, *Breviceps fuscus*;
Plaintive Rain Frog, *Breviceps verrucosus*;
Spotted Rain Frog, *Breviceps maculatus*;
Strawberry Rain Frog, *Breviceps acutirostris*;
Transvaal Forest Rain Frog, *Breviceps sylvestris*

**Size:** 35–55 mm.

**Description:** Almost spherical body with the head barely protruding and legs shorter than the body length. Granular^G skin. Brown or grey with black markings. Belly granular white with grey markings. Toes stubby with no webbing. Bears a large digging tubercle^G on the heel. Pupils horizontal.

**Where found:** Forest floor, sometimes emerging into adjacent grassland or fynbos^G.

**Call:** Burred, slow whistles or chirrups, especially in a mist or during soft rain.

**Reproduction:** Males are glued to the back of the females with an adhesive secretion while mating. Eggs are laid in burrows in the forest floor. Tadpoles develop within the burrow and only emerge as fully formed froglets.

**Notes:** The different species^G inhabit different areas of forest.

*Plaintive Rain Frog*

# Bushveld Rain Frogs

*Breviceps* sp.

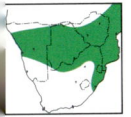

**This group includes:** Bushveld Rain Frog, *Breviceps adspersus;* Mozambique Rain Frog, *Breviceps mossambicus*

**Size:** 40–50 mm.

**Description:** Stubby body; very short legs and head. Skin rough, granular$^G$. Mottled brown with pairs of yellow-brown patches. Belly smooth white. Male throat black; female throat mottled. Toes stubby with no webbing. Large digging tubercle$^G$ on the heel. Pupils horizontal.

**Where found:** Bushveld$^G$ savanna$^G$, sandy soils. Bushveld Rain Frog prefers dryer lowlands, Mozambique Rain Frog rocky, grassy slopes, high escarpments.

**Call:** Two or three burred whistles followed by a pause.

**Reproduction:** Males glued to the back of females while mating. Eggs are laid in underground burrows. Tadpoles emerge from burrows as fully formed froglets.

**Notes:** Puff themselves into an almost spherical ball when alarmed. Very incompetent swimmers; will inflate themselves and bob about until they drift to the bank if they fall into water.

*Bushveld Rain Frog*

# Cape Rain Frog

*Breviceps gibbosus*

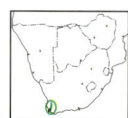

**Size:** 50–60 mm.

**Description:** Rotund body with barely protruding head, legs shorter than the body length. Granular<sup>G</sup> skin; brown with cream. Belly rough skinned; mottled brown on cream. Male throat granular. Toes stubby with no webbing. Bears a large digging tubercle<sup>G</sup> on the heel. Pupils horizontal.

**Where found:** Burrows near bushes or logs in fynbos<sup>G</sup> and suburban gardens.

**Call:** A harsh squawk repeated at irregular intervals.

**Reproduction:** Males are glued to the back of the females while mating. Eggs are laid in underground burrows. Tadpoles develop within the nest and only emerge once they are fully formed froglets.

**Notes:** This was the first South African species<sup>G</sup> to be scientifically described, in 1758. Like all rain frogs, they are able to inflate themselves into a ball when alarmed, making themselves appear much larger than they really are to a predator. This has earned them the Afrikaans name 'Blaasop'.

# Desert Rain Frog

*Breviceps macrops*

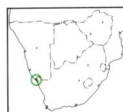

**Size:** 40–50 mm.

**Description:** Smooth, flabby body. Yellowish cream with a brown M-pattern behind the very large eyes. Belly skin thin, translucent. Chest pure white. Toes stubby with thick webbing that enables them to walk on loose sand. Large digging tubercle<sup>G</sup> on the heel. Pupils horizontal.

**Where found:** Desert and coastal sand dunes.

**Call:** A long, clear whistle. Squeals when handled.

**Reproduction:** Not known, but probably a similar process to that of other Rain Frogs.

**Notes:** The dunes in which it occurs are being strip-mined for diamonds and the species<sup>G</sup> may soon become extinct.

# Banded Rubber Frog

*Phrynomantis bifasciatus*

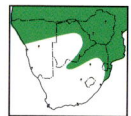

**Size:** 50–65 mm

**Description:** Smooth, shiny black or dark grey body with two broad, reddish stripes running from the snout along the sides; large reddish spot on the rump. Belly grey, covered with a number of white spots. Toes without webbing. Pupils circular.

**Where found:** Banks of savanna$^G$ pans$^G$. During the day they hide in tree holes and similar retreats.

**Call:** Beautiful, melodious, two-second trills every few seconds.

**Reproduction:** Eggs are attached to surface vegetation. Tadpoles reach 35 mm; transparent except for the tail which has red and black markings and a thin, whip-like tip. They feed by filtering plankton$^G$ from the water.

**Notes:** A toxic$^G$ substance is secreted from the skin to deter predators. It is harmless to humans unless eaten, but take care to keep it away from eyes, mouth and open wounds. Wash well after handling the frog.

# Platannas

*Xenopus* sp.

**This group includes:**
Cape Platanna *Xenopus gilli*
Common Platanna, *Xenopus laevis*; Tropical Platanna, *Xenopus muelleri*; Cape Platanna *Xenopus gilli*

**Size:** 40–100 mm

**Description:** Body streamlined and slippery. Grey or brown, mottled. Eyes positioned on the top of the head, looking upwards. Sensory organs appear like stitches along the sides of the body. Belly off-white or yellow, sometimes spotted. Toes fully webbed, three with hard claws. Pupils circular.

**Where found:** Any reasonably permanent body of water. Remains submerged except for rare migrations overland.

**Call:** Underwater buzzing or tapping sounds.

*Common Platanna*

**Reproduction:** Breeding pairs perform elaborate underwater acrobatics while depositing eggs on aquatic[G] vegetation. Tadpoles reach 25 mm; transparent. Hang head down in the water while filtering plankton[G].

**Notes:** The only southern African frogs that eat underwater. They swallow living and non-living food, pushing it into their mouths with their forelimbs. They are used extensively as laboratory animals. The Cape Platanna is being threatened by the destruction of its habitat[G] on the Cape Flats and by competition from the Common Platanna.

# Common River Frog

*Afrana angolensis*

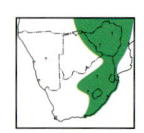

**Size:** 40–80 mm.

**Description:** Body angular with a sharp nose – eyes bulge beyond the outline of the head when viewed from above. Green or brown, often with dark spots and a vertebral<sup>G</sup> stripe. Belly smooth white, sometimes with dark markings. Legs long – shank<sup>G</sup> more than half the length of the body. Toes long, webbed. Pupils horizontal.

**Where found:** Grassland streams and other permanent bodies of water.

**Call:** A sharp rattle followed by a croak; 'kikikikik-kereooooow'.

**Reproduction:** Eggs are laid in shallow water on the bottom of streams or dams. Tadpoles reach 100 mm; mottled brown with white belly. Metamorphosis<sup>G</sup> sometimes takes more than a year to complete.

**Notes:** Common River Frogs are often found along the banks of streams or dams and plop into the water when they are approached. They usually swim quickly to the bottom and kick up a puff of detritus to disguise their position. After a few minutes they resurface some distance away.

# Cape River Frog

*Afrana fuscigula*

**Size:** 60–120 mm.

**Description:** Similar to the Common River Frog. Body angular – eyes do not bulge beyond the outline of the head when viewed from above. Green or brown, often with dark spots and a stripe down the back. Belly smooth white with dark markings. Legs long – shank<sup>G</sup> more than half the length of the body. Toes long, webbed. Pupils horizontal.

**Where found:** Rivers, streams and dams in fynbos<sup>G</sup> and grassland.

**Call:** A series of taps, lasting for about ten seconds, followed by a loud groan – slower and longer than the call of the Common River Frog.

**Reproduction:** Eggs laid in shallow water. Tadpoles reach 150 mm; mottled brown with white belly. Metamorphosis<sup>G</sup> often takes more than a year.

**Notes:** River Frogs appear to be dispersing further northwards. This is because of the growing number of farm dams being built across the country, which River Frogs tend to colonise as they are ideal breeding sites for this species<sup>G</sup>.

# Ornate Frog

*Hildebrandtia ornata*

**Size:** 55–65 mm.

**Description:** Square, thickset body. Variations of green, black and golden brown stripes or patches on the back and flanks. Belly smooth white. Throat black with two off-white Y-shaped stripes. Male vocal sacs<sup>G</sup> in pouches under each side of the jaw. Legs long – shank<sup>G</sup> more than half the length of the body. Toes webbed. Pupils horizontal.

**Where found:** In the shallow water at the edges of savanna<sup>G</sup> pans<sup>G</sup> and vleis<sup>G</sup>.

**Call:** A prolonged, nasal squawk.

**Reproduction:** Eggs are laid in shallow water on the bottom of streams or dams. Tadpoles reach 90 mm; dark brown with a white belly. Fully grown tadpoles show Y shapes under the throat that are visible in adult frogs.

**Notes:** Little is known about these frogs because they remain buried for most of the year and only emerge to breed during the rainy season.

# Plain Grass Frog

*Ptychadena anchietae*

**Size:** 40–55 mm.

**Description:** Plain brick-red with a pale triangle on the snout which is sharp. Six ridges run from the snout down the length of the body. No light vertebral[G] stripe. Belly smooth white with a yellow tinge. Male vocal sacs[G] in pouches under each side of the jaw. Legs long and powerful – shank[G] more than half the length of the body. Toes webbed. Pupils horizontal.

**Where found:** The shallow water at the edges of savanna[G] pans[G] and vleis[G].

**Call:** A high pitched trill repeated rapidly, about three trills per second.

**Reproduction:** Eggs float on the surface of the water. Tadpoles reach 45 mm; grey with a transparent belly.

**Notes:** The call is one of the typical sounds of a bushveld[G] night, but is seldom identified as being that of a frog. During the day they hide away among tussocks of grass near water, moving to the water's edge to call at dusk. Unlike river and stream frogs, they usually jump away from the water if disturbed, not into it.

# Sharp-nosed Grass Frog

*Ptychadena oxyrhynchus*

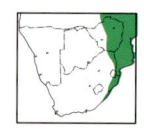

**Size:** 50–60 mm.

**Description:** Mottled grey and brown with black spots and a pale triangle on the snout, which is sharp. Six ridges run down the length of the back. No light vertebral[G] stripe. Belly is smooth, white with a yellow tinge. Male vocal sacs[G] in pouches under each side of the jaw. Legs long and powerful – shank[G] more than half the length of the body. Toes webbed. Pupils horizontal.

**Where found:** The shallow water at the edges of savanna[G] pans[G] and vleis[G].

**Call:** A high pitched trill repeated slowly once or twice and followed by a pause.

**Reproduction:** Eggs stay afloat along the surface of the water. Tadpoles reach 55 mm; grey with black mottling.

**Notes:** Holds the world record for the longest jump (*Guinness Book of Records*). The official measurement is calculated by adding together the distance covered in three consecutive jumps. The record stands at 10.3 m. It was achieved on 21 May 1977 in Paulpietersburg and has never been equalled, even at the Angel's Camp Jumping Frog Jubilee which is held every year in Calaveras County, California.

# Broad-banded Grass Frog

*Ptychadena mossambica*

**Size:** 40–50 mm.

**Description:** Sharp snout. Six ridges run down the back. Greenish grey with spots. A broad, pale stripe from snout to rump. Belly smooth, white with yellow tinge. Male vocal sacs<sup>G</sup> in pouches under each side of the jaw. Legs long and powerful - shank<sup>G</sup> more than half the length of the body. Toes webbed. Pupils horizontal.

**Where found:** In water-logged grass surrounding savanna<sup>G</sup> pans<sup>G</sup> and vleis<sup>G</sup>.

**Call:** A harsh, nasal quacking.

**Reproduction:** Not known, but probably a similar process to that of other Grass Frogs.

**Notes:** The call can easily be mistaken for ducks in the wetland. Unlike other grass frogs, they keep themselves concealed in the grass while calling, even after dark.

# Giant Bullfrog

*Pyxicephalus adspersus*

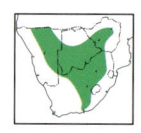

**Size:** 110–200 mm.

**Description:** Heavy, flabby body. Olive green with ridges of whitish skin; no patterning on the face. Orange in groin and armpits. Juveniles bright green and black. Belly smooth, creamy yellow. Toes webbed, bears a large digging tubercle<sup>G</sup> on the heel. Usually waddles and only jumps when being aggressive. Pupils horizontal.

**Where found:** Shallow, rain-filled pools in grassland and dry savanna<sup>G</sup>. It remains buried in a cocoon for most of the year and is usually only seen during the breeding season.

**Call:** A deep, slow bellow which sounds very much like the lowing of cattle.

**Reproduction:** Eggs laid after heavy rains. Males fight vigorously at the breeding site. Tadpoles form large, compact swarms and reach 75 mm. Males guard the tadpoles and dig escape channels to other pools if the water starts to dry up.

**Notes:** The largest southern African frog. Eats small birds, rodents and other frogs. Two fang-like projections in the lower jaw are used for holding prey and for fighting.

# African Bullfrog

*Pyxicephalus edulus*

**Size:** 90–110 mm.

**Description:** Dull green with brown mottling. Bears ridges of whitish skin and sometimes a vertebral<sup>G</sup> stripe. Mottled pattern extends onto the face. Juveniles are bright green and black. Belly is smooth, creamy yellow. Toes webbed, bears a large digging tubercle<sup>G</sup> on the heel. Pupils horizontal.

**Where found:** Shallow, rain-filled pools in lowveld<sup>G</sup> and savanna<sup>G</sup>. Remains buried for most of the year and usually only seen during the breeding season.

**Call:** A short, low-pitched yapping.

**Reproduction:** Eggs and tadpoles are similar to those of the Giant Bullfrog but aggression at the breeding site is generally less intense.

**Notes:** This species<sup>G</sup>, together with the Giant Bullfrog, is frequently eaten by local people. When large numbers of newly metamorphosed<sup>G</sup> frogs emerge from the water the larger ones often devour the smaller ones. This greatly increases their rate of growth and thus their chances of survival.

# Striped Stream Frogs

*Strongylopus* sp.

**This group includes:** Striped Stream Frog, *Strongylopus fasciatus*; Banded Stream Frog, *Strongylopus bonaespei*

**Size:** 35–45 mm.

**Description:** Sharply angular body with pointed nose. Yellow and dark brown stripes with a broad vertebral[G] stripe. Belly smooth, white. Male throat yellow. Shank[G] longer than half the body. Very long toes, slightly webbed. Pupils horizontal.

**Where found:** Thick grass adjacent to streams and dams as well as marshy areas in mountain fynbos[G].

**Call:** A sharp, piercing 'pip' uttered singly or in a short burst of four or five. Choruses of males sound like twittering birds. Banded Stream Frog gives a harsh crackle.

**Reproduction:** Eggs are laid in pools of water. Tadpoles reach 70 mm; brown stippled[G] with a black tail tip.

**Notes:** Calling persists in autumn and early winter. It is heard far less frequently in the warmer months.

*Striped Stream Frog*

# Clicking Stream Frog

*Strongylopus grayii*

**Size:** 35–45 mm.

**Description:** Angular body. Wide variation in colour; usually has dark spots on a grey background and may have a broad or narrow coloured vertebral[G] stripe. Belly smooth, white. Male throat has a slight gold sheen. Shank[G] longer than half the body. Long toes webbed. Pupils horizontal.

**Where found:** Grassland and fynbos[G]. Breeds in a variety of habitats[G] from cold, high altitude sponges to vleis[G], slow-moving streams or brackish seaside pools.

**Call:** A sharp snap like the clicking of one's tongue, rapidly repeated. Choruses of males give a crackling sound.

**Reproduction:** Eggs laid in damp soil next to the water. Tadpoles reach 60 mm; black with white underside.

**Notes:** Eggs are able to tolerate long periods of drought and, even if partly dried out, they hatch successfully when next exposed to rain. Within its range this is one of the most common species[G] and the persistent clicking call can be heard around any wetland.

# Sand Frogs

*Tomopterna* sp.

**This group includes:**
Cape Sand Frog, *Tomopterna delalandii*;
Knocking Sand Frog, *Tomopterna krugerensis*;
Natal Sand Frog, *Tomopterna natalensis*;
Russetbacked Sand Frog, *Tomopterna marmorata*;
Tandy's Sand Frog, *Tomopterna tandyi*;
Tremolo Sand Frog, *Tomopterna cryptotus*;
Beaded Sand Frog, *Tomopterna tuberculosa*

*Tremolo Sand Frog*

**Size:** 45–50 mm.

**Description:** Stockily built with lumpy skin and a pale ridge running from the jaw to the armpit. Mottled brown, grey or russet with a butterfly-shaped patch between the shoulders. Sometimes has stripes on the back. Belly is smooth, white with grey under the jaw. Toes are webbed. Bears a conspicuous digging tubercle[G] on the heel. Pupils horizontal.

**Where found:** Sandy or muddy banks around pans[G], temporary rain pools and vleis[G] in savanna[G] and grassland. Spend much of the time in underground burrows.

**Call:** Rapidly repeated, sharp notes or tapping sounds. Differs markedly between species[G].

**Reproduction:** Eggs laid on the mud floor of shallow water. Tadpoles reach 35 mm; dark brown, fat bodied with a short tail.

**Notes:** They use their hind legs to shuffle backwards under the soil where they spend daylight hours and much of the dry season.

# Hogsback Frog

*Anhydrophryne rattrayi*

**Size:** 20–22 mm.

**Description:** Small, delicate body. Brick red to dark brown, sometimes with a vertebral<sup>G</sup> stripe. Black 'mask' runs from snout through eye to shoulder. Male's snout is hard, sharp and colourless. Belly white with dark mottling. Toes without webbing. Pupils horizontal.

**Where found:** Damp, mossy seepage near streams and in the Amatola mountain forests.

**Call:** Clear, melodious cheeps repeated incessantly.

**Reproduction:** The male uses the hardened tip of his snout to dig an underground chamber about 25 mm in diameter. Once he has attracted the female by his call, the mating pair enter the chamber where the eggs are laid. Here they develop into fully formed froglets that emerge after four weeks.

**Notes:** Although restricted to a small range, it is common in the Hogsback area and calling can be heard throughout a summer day, especially in the vicinity of waterfalls.

# Chirping Frogs

*Arthroleptella* sp.

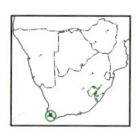

**This group includes:**
Bainskloof Chirping Frog, *Arthroleptella bicolor*;
Cape Chirping Frog, *Arthroleptella lightfooti*;
Drewes's Chirping Frog, *Arthroleptella drewsii*;
Mist Belt Chirping Frog, *Arthroleptella ngongoniensis*;
Natal Chirping Frog, *Arthroleptella hewitti*;
Villiers's Chirping Frog, *Arthroleptella villiersi*

**Size:** 20–22 mm.

**Description:** Delicate bodies. Extremely variable in colour, from pale greenish brown to blue-black. Sometimes has a vertebral[G] stripe. Belly colour is variable, from pure white to mottled to black, but it has no distinct spots as in the Cacos. Toes are without webbing. Pupils horizontal.

**Where found:** Damp leaves and moss in seepages or muddy banks

*Natal Chirping Frog*

near mountain streams in forests, fynbos[G] or grassland.

**Call:** High-pitched chirps that differ only slightly between the various species[G].

**Reproduction:** Eggs laid on damp moss. Tadpoles colourless with dark tails. They squirm about on the moss until they develop into frogs.

**Notes:** Most species are indistinguishable from each other except by laboratory analysis.

**50**

# Common Caco

*Cacosternum boettgeri*

**Size:** 20–25 mm.

**Description:** Small, slightly flattened bodies. Extremely variable colours and patterns, from bright green to brown and a variety of stripes and spots. Belly is white with grey spots. Toes are without webbing. Pupils horizontal.

**Where found:** Marshland, inundated grass around temporary rain pools and ditches.

**Call:** Explosive bursts of six to ten clicks, almost painful to the human ear at close quarters.

**Reproduction:** Eggs laid in small clusters on underwater plants. Tadpoles reach 30 mm. Pale brown, partially transparent with a striped head and white belly.

**Notes:** The wide diversity of colours helps to confuse predators which may become accustomed to hunting frogs of one particular colour.
To generate so loud a call, this very small frog has a vocal sac[G] that expands to almost half the size of the frog itself.

# Bronze Caco

*Cacosternum nanum*

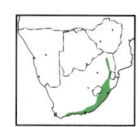

**Size:** 20–25 mm.

**Description:** Small, slightly flattened bodies. Various shades of brown with symmetrical dark flecks. Marked by a well-defined, dark facial 'mask'. Belly is white with black spots that are more densely distributed on the chest and throat. Toes are without webbing. Pupils horizontal.

**Where found:** In vleis<sup>G</sup>, rain pools and roadside ditches.

**Call:** A short, repeated, creaking chirp, interspersed with clicking.

**Reproduction:** Eggs and tadpoles are indistinguishable from the Common Caco.

**Notes:** Calling can be heard from almost every ditch on warm days after rain but the frogs are remarkably difficult to find.

# Kloof Frog

*Natalobatrachus bonebergi*

**Size:** 30–35 mm.

**Description:** Angular body with a sharply pointed snout bearing a pale triangle on top. Grey-brown with a central stripe of variable colour and often a narrow stripe within the broader one. Belly is off-white with dark flecks. Toes are webbed, bear large T-shaped adhesive pads at the tips. Pupils horizontal.

**Where found:** Deep forest gorges where there are damp cliffs and slow-moving sections of streams.

**Call:** A very soft click at irregular intervals.

**Reproduction:** Eggs laid in stiff cakes of jelly, hidden in inaccessible places overhanging the water. As tadpoles mature the jelly softens and they slide into the water. Tadpoles reach 40 mm; grey with a colourless tail.

**Notes:** Sightings of this frog are unusual because of its quiet call and remote habitat[G]. The wide adhesive toe-pads enable the frog to climb vertical, slippery rock faces into positions that are inaccessible to predators.

# Snoring Puddle Frog

*Phrynobatrachus natalensis*

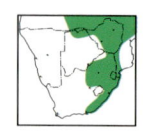

**Size:** 25–30 mm.

**Description:** Small, stocky body with lumpy skin. Mottled grey or brown, often with a broad or narrow vertebral[G] stripe. Belly is smooth, off-white with grey flecks. Male vocal sac[G] is black and folds into creases on either side of the jaw. Toes webbed. Pupils horizontal.

**Where found:** Vleis[G], grassy pans[G] and shallows around farm dams.

**Call:** A rapidly repeated nasal snoring.

**Reproduction:** Eggs float on the water in a single-layered patch.

Tadpoles reach 35 mm; light brown with black stippling on the transparent tail.

**Notes:** Very common throughout its range. Because of its variable colour it may be confused with river or stream frogs, however its snout is much shorter. It may also be confused with small toads, but it does not bear parotid glands[G].

# Foam Nest Frog

*Chiromantis xerampelina*

**Size:** 50–90 mm.

**Description:** Large, rough-skinned body with long, pliant legs. Grey or tan, sometimes with indistinct spots and markings. Becomes almost white in the sunlight. Belly has pinkish-grey, granular[G] skin with a speckled throat. Toes webbed and bear adhesive discs at the tips for climbing. Pupils horizontal.

**Where found:** Trees near bushveld[G] pans[G].

**Call:** Soft, discordant croaks.

**Reproduction:** Eggs laid in large foam nests on branches overhanging water. Foam is generated by groups of males churning the egg jelly with their hind legs. Hatching tadpoles fall from the nest into the water below. Tadpoles reach 50 mm, dark brown.

**Notes:** Nests are a common sight in trees which overhang pans in the bushveld. Foam insulates eggs from the heat and cold, keeping them moist and safe from predators.

# Glossary

**Aquatic** – living in water.
**Asperities** – small, pimple-like elevations on the skin.
**Bushveld** – open woodland typical of southern and central Africa.
**Fynbos** – the flora of the Cape, composed largely of Ericas, Proteas and Restios.
**Glandular** – bearing skin glands that secrete fluids.
**Granular** – grainy or pebble-like surface of the skin.
**Habitat** – the type of place in which an animal occurs naturally.
**Hybridise** – two different species inter-breeding with each other.
**Lowveld** – warm and humid low altitude regions on the east of southern Africa.
**Marbled** – veined or dappled skin markings resembling marble.
**Metamorphosis** – transformation from tadpole to adult frog.
**Pan** – water-filled depression not fed or drained by a watercourse.
**Parotid glands** – pair of oval-shaped glands situated on the neck behind the eyes of most species of toads.

*Tinker Reed Frog*

**Plankton** – microscopic plants and animals suspended in water.
**Savanna** – open woodland (see also Bushveld[G]).
**Shank** – tibia or shin bone – the longest section of the frog's leg.
**Species** – population that breeds naturally with one another and produces viable offspring.
**Stipples** – dotted patterning on the skin.
**Toxic** – poisonous or noxious.
**Tubercle** – flap or nodule of hardened tissue for digging.
**Vertebral** – running down the line of the spine.
**Vertebrate** – animal with a spinal column.
**Vlei** – widening of a stream to form a marshy area.
**Vocal sac** – chamber of elastic skin under the throat that is inflated as the male frog calls.